Shit House Rat

Poems by Daniel Crocker

Kansas City   Spartan Press   Missouri

Spartan Press
Kansas City, Missouri
spartanpresskc.com

Copyright (c) 2017 Daniel Crocker
First Edition 1 3 5 7 9 10 8 6 4 2
ISBN: 978-1-946642-29-5
LCCN: 2017953927

Edits, design and layout: Jason Ryberg
Cover art: Ashley Crocker
Author photo: The author
All rights reserved. No part of this publication may be reproduced or transmitted in any form or by any means, electronic or mechanical, including photocopying, recording or by info retrieval system, without prior written permission from the author.

ACKNOWLEDGMENTS

Spartan Press would like to thank Prospero's Books,
The Prospero Institute of Disquieted P/o/e/t/i/c/s,
The Fellowship of N-Finite Jest, Jeanette Powers, j.d.tulloch,
Jason Preu, The Osage Arts Community and The Robert J.
Deuser Foundation For Libertarian Studies.

Some of these poems and essays have appeared in: *The Chiron Review, The Mas Tequila Review, The Kentucky Review,* all the reviews, *We Want Insanity, Clockwise Cat, Joey and the Blackboots, Rusty Truck, Fried Chicken and Coffee* and *Drunk Monkeys* and the chapbook *The One Where I Ruin Your Childhood* (Sundress Publications)

CONTENTS

Hey Graziano! Yeah, Crocker? Have You Heard?
    What's that, Dan? It's Over, Man / 1

Some Fava Beans / 4

Growing Up / 6

Snuffleupagas / 8

Recipe for Delicious Pot Roast and
    Mess Free Suicide / 10

They Haven't Called It a Complex
    in Forty Years / 12

I Married a Sling Blade / 16

A Brief Statement From Kurt Cobain's Gun / 19

Who's Happy Here Tonight? / 20

How Me and Lord Byron Got our
    Grooves Back / 22

Eat / 25

I Wouldn't Mind You Crazy if You Didn't
  Get So Damned Depressed About It / 27

Dear Nerd, In Regards to Your Nerd Query / 28

Brutal / 30

Elmo Goes Emo / 34

C is for Cookie / 35

A Dream of Siblings / 37

City of Bones / 40

I Don't Write Political Poems (On the Eve
  of a Government Shutdown) / 44

My Mother Calls / 47

Spirit Animal: Margot Tenenbaum / 50

Welcome to Fantasy Island / 52

Don't Kill Self / 55

Jazz / 56

George Bailey's Blues / 62

Full Moon / 65

I'm Going to Kill Myself Tomorrow / 67

I Like To Cut Myself / 68

The Normals / 70

Pill / 72

Elton and George / 73

Take a Moment / 75

I Wish / 76

In Response to the Article "10 People to Rid
   Yourself of Before the New Year" / 78

Dinged / 80

You Better Fucking Believe There's a Monster
   at the End of This Book / 83

Daniel Crocker: An Introduction

I'm showing my age. I've been reading the work of Daniel Crocker for the better part of 20 years, since the days of presses with names like Alpha Beat and Green Bean, those years now long gone, spent waiting by the mailbox for letters from all over the country and feeling like maybe you were the only one out there scribbling words on faded register receipts or on the surface of some wilted onion paper fed into the mouth of a hungry typewriter. Years spent laboring in dish rooms, gas stations, and fast food joints looking for a way to work out your own insanity. Dan would be the first person to tell you that he's a little crazy, out there on the edge with the rest of us, leaving it all on the page.

What has always set Dan's writing apart from your average small press poet, aside from the fact that it's actually good, is that the man is versatile, I mean he can write anything, from pop culture homages to He-Man and the McRib to quiet moments of darkness spent bathing in the moonlight of his own flaws, and no matter what the subject is, it all feels like high art, whatever that means. It all comes across more than ever in this latest volume wisely published by Kansas City's Spartan Press.

This book simply has brains as big as its heart.
I'm glad Dan and I met when we did, Cobain's corpse still warm in the ground, it just feels like a better time now, a time with something to say, Dan has never been short of words, if you're just getting to know his work, I'd say you have some catching up to do, and when you're done, his scars will still feel as fresh as they did in 1995, I promise you.

—John Dorsey

*For Nate and Margaret
and a special thanks to
James Brubaker for all
his suggestions*

Hey Graziano! Yeah, Crocker? Have You Heard?
What's that, Dan? It's Over, Man.

It's over, I say, it's over
I'm going to kill myself tomorrow
I woke up with a panic attack again

My wife squeezes my left nipple
hard

Dear God, I say
your fingers are like talons

Well, she wants to know, are you
thinking about something
else at least?

I tell her about
when I was a kid
a time of quiet minds
that doesn't even seem real
anymore

My cousin used to make
fun of me because I was
too fat to climb a tree
So I decided to show
that little bastard what
was what

I went out back to
his favorite climbing tree--
the big one--
ripped off my Frankie Says Relax T-Shirt
like Hulk Hogan and
pulled strength from a well
of willpower I didn't know existed
I embraced my destiny

I made it about
six inches up
before sliding down
like a fireman and
ripping off a nipple
against the bark

Took it off like sandpaper
I said
Margaret pinched it again
gentle this time
It's there now, she says

Sure, I say, but from eight
to seventeen, I was a one nipple
wonder
It came back about the time
I grew my rad mullet

We both know
I'm not really
thinking about anything else
I only tell this story
so she'll rest her head
on my chest again

Sometimes, I still feel it
like an amputee might
I say, as she falls back to sleep

My ghost nipple
a memory
crying out
right where the new   *There's something really bad*
one is.   *coming at the end of this book,*
                               Bird.

Some Fava Beans

Years of heavy drinking
finally caught up with me
so I went to my doctor
for one of those new livers

*That's a preexisting
condition.
Bird, we're not going
to cover that.*

He had a nice healthy one
in a jar on his desk
I'd had my eye on it for months

Gimmie that liver, I said

Sorry, he said, that liver's taken

I couldn't believe it

Yep, son, that liver there
belongs to Mickey Mantle
I don't mind telling you
I'm a pretty big fan

Mickey goddamned Mantle

*Helloooooooo?
This is Bird. Who
said that? Who wants to
come out and play?*

He's got to be at least 110, man

Oh, he's been dead for years
the doctor said

I've got two kids
I need that good, brown liver

Maybe you shouldn't drink so much
then, the doctor said

Me? What about Mickey
goddamned Mantle?

Nothing I can do, the doctor said

                                            Helloooooo?

I've got a nice spleen out back
if you want it, a couple of kidneys
I could make a deal on

but this liver is going
to The Mick

He's a national treasure
He married a model
He's been to the White House
seven or eight times
What have you done?
I'm a poet, I say

Kid, get the hell out
of my office. And do us
both a favor, don't   *Helloooooo?*
come back.

                                    You know who this is.
                                    Sure, let's play.

Growing Up

I saw the Cold War
Hell, it was no Vietnam
but it was something

I saw Silence
equal death
and stayed silent
anyway

We watched "The Day After"
We watched "Roots"

Every special news break
        we lost our faces
        shuddered
sure of annihilation

They wanted to put Reagan's goddamned
face on a mountain and I
missed Haley's Comet for this

II

I was neurotic
in heat with religion
dry humping the word

When I sinned I prayed
Dear God, please forgive me
for all of my sins

When others sinned I prayed
Dear God, please forgive me   *Bird? Tear down*
for all of my sins   *that wall, Bird. Bird*
    tear down that wall.

If I thought of sin I prayed
Dear God, please forgive me
for all my sins

Sesame Street Ronald Reagan MTV   *Are the night mares*
Sesame Street Ronald Reagan and MTV   *back, Bird? Are your*
What have you done to your weary   *glowing nightmares back?*
ragged, holy boys?

Snuffleupagas

Well, Snuffy, you really pulled a fast one
You convinced us all that you didn't exist
There has to be a trick to it, right
a little sleight of hand
I'd like to know

What are you so depressed about anyway
they have pills for that
even on your street

And would it have been so bad if you only
existed in the mind of one gloriously joyful
bird? You could have wrapped yourself around
him like a scarf. You could have
given him the gravitas he so desperately
needed

You were such a great metaphor   *I'm no metaphor, asshole.*

But then you had to go and be real
You wake us from our happy dream
face dragging
Do you know what, Bird,
Nietzsche was right. Everyone dies alone.
I know, I know

It's all meaningless, Bird.
I've been reading Schopenhauer.
Want to hear my thoughts on marriage?

You need help.

I'm fine, Bird, I'm fine.

I don't believe you.

Recipe for Delicious Pot Roast and Mess Free Suicide

Lay down a blanket
of Shamwows on the kitchen floor
With eleven pounds of premium
chuck roast
you'll want to give yourself
five or six hours

Take a gallon sized
freezer bag —
Ziplock because life
can be pretty messy —
and place it on the counter

Cover the meat in water
Throw in a fucking onion
if you want

Heat to a boil

Or fuck it. I'm not
here to tell you how
to kill yourself
I got my own problems

Is Trump the Devil?

*Does he look like
the Devil, Bird?*

*Everyone looks like the
Devil, Snuffy.*

I can't stop saying Devil now.

It's okay. It's okay.

Devil, Devil, Devil!

That's right. That's right!

They Haven't Called It a Complex in Forty Years

My wife thinks I should see
a psychiatrist about it
and leave her the hell alone

So, I do. He has
a list of questions for me
He asks if I'm
straight or gay

A little bit of both, I say

What, he asks
like he's Frank Nelson

A fat wooden cross covers
half a wall. A Samurai sword hangs
on another. There's a Bible
on his desk

He scribbles
something onto his notepad

I ask if everything
is okay

Yes, he says
It's just that

this is exciting. I've never
met one before

One what, I want to know
One of you, he says
I mean the boy version

He asks about my wife
my job, my kids
but, oddly enough,
never about my mother

When he's done
We sit in silence
staring at each other
It would become a habit
of ours

Finally, he asks if I'm depressed
No more than any other poet, I say

He doesn't find it
funny

Close your eyes, he says
Breath deep. Imagine
you're in the final match of a big
karate tournament

This is kind of like that

No time for jokes

For three years
this guy never made
a metaphor that didn't
have karate in it

He fancied them parables

So, he says, what do you
think is wrong with you
Frankly, I say, I don't think
it's any of my goddamn business

I guess he tried
It couldn't have been fun
for him either

He really only ever
gave me one piece of advice
At night, he said, think about
a lake. The moon is full
The water gently laps
against the shore
The music of the frogs
and crickets lull you off to sleep

He had a real way with words

Look, I don't know if

he had actually ever been camping
but I know that

I fucking hate lakes
the mud
the leeches
the things that brush
against you beneath
the deep, filthy
water.   *It's going to get worse, Bird.*
　　　　　　　Don't say it, Snuffy.
　　　　　There's a monster coming.

I Married a Sling Blade

We're watching Sling Blade
and I'm laughing my ass off
Margaret says, I don't think
it's supposed to be so funny

Doyle pushes some dude in a wheelchair
into the wall and he splays
like a crash test dummy
                      dot dot dot like the poets do

It's not funny Margaret says

That Frank, he lives inside of his own heart

Holy Christ, I say
one minute Karl doesn't know
where he is
the next he's spouting poetry

That's you, Margaret says
I married a fucking Sling Blade

Then we're both laughing
but later I think
maybe she's right
She works in mental health
after all
As did I once

All I remember

> There was Carol who spoke to the Raspberry Spirits.
> There was Mike who showed me the peppermint god breaking through the violent clouds like a fist.
> There was Joe who thought he was Jesus and spat in my face as a blessing. When he tried to stab me with a pencil I grabbed his wrist. It was as soft as a petal and as delicate as a pistil.
> There was Leigh the Magdalene who wouldn't shit. We held her down, someone, possibly me, had to stick his finger into the dark spider hole of her ass to see if she was impacted and maybe I imagined myself going through a tunnel like a death vision and speaking in tongues from her mouth,

a ghost.

> There was Teresa, who Marvin, close to retiring, headbutted when she refused her meds. I kissed the wound and left with bloody lips.

Well, if I'm a Sling Blade
I guess I'm a Sling Blade
I laugh at all the things that
aren't funny. Like the dead
poets. The dead relatives. All the
goddamned lead.

> Leigh said, Jesus doesn't want me to have a bowel movement. He hates filth.
> Shh, I said, stroking her long gray hair. It's the filth He loves the most. He rolls in it like a dog.

If I could do the voice
The Sling Blade voice
the beautiful things I would say.
But eventually, it has to stop, right,
You got voices, all right.

the saying of all these things?

A Brief Statement From Kurt Cobain's Gun

Thank you all for coming. First, I'd like to say that I am deeply sorry for my actions. However, I'd like to make it clear that I didn't mean to kill him. Like many of you, I also think he had a few good years left. Of course, I can understand your skepticism. I am, after all, a gun. Then again, I don't kill people. You all kill people. And what was I supposed to do when he placed his mouth against mine, his toe curled around my trigger? My sleek body was built to fire. Am I to blame if all I could think, in my ecstasy, was pull, damn it, *pull!*

Who's Happy Here Tonight?
for Lexapro

Certainly not the chopped up pig
boiling in the pot of beans
in the kitchen

Not the guy whose throat
is raw again from smoking

Not the woman asleep in the bedroom
or the husband who hasn't fucked
her in months

Some nights I'm so sure I will
die here, stoned and wondering
if my neighbors can smell it
and one day I will

feel their footsteps above me
a rattle in my chest

but for now

The only one happy
tonight is the poem
the bees thank you
the rattling pipes thank you
the fat engagement ring on the finger

of this hot mama thanks
you Anheuser-Busch thanks you
Doe Run thanks you, boys of lice
and lean faces thank you
your ridiculous call to beauty
the red pepper
added to the boiling pot
thanks you, but not me.
Not me and not the pig.   *Nor me, Bird, nor
me.*

How Me and Lord Byron Got our Grooves Back

I'm having beers
with Warren Zevon
We're talking
about our cancers   *Don't forget dad and sis, Bird.*

It's boring
I may not even have
cancer
Warren certainly doesn't

He wants
to invite Kerouac
but I'm tired
and Kerouac
cries into his whiskey
and it always ends when he
demands to be draped in
an American Flag and buried
up north

I was tired of every thing
at that point
in the deep south
so many miles from my wife
and Adrienne Rich rebuffing
my every advance

Let me show you how it's done
Byron says
I don't know where he came
from but his entrance a
dramatic flapping of a cape
was something to behold

What else can I do
I sit back and watch
It's impressive. You'd think
him a young David Lee Roth
In the end, however,
It doesn't go any better
for him that it did me

Tonight, Adrienne says
no poetry will serve
and that seems to be the gist
of the whole goddamned thing

All of us brooding on the mistakes
we just can't seem to write our way
out of
those long haul problems
stretch out like the Mississippi
waters the deep troubled waters
the anxieties of speaking

The things hidden so well
no one can fault you for them
clasped so tightly no one would
bother to steal them and even if
they did what could they do

We find some joy in that
and a few other things
and think maybe we should
invite old Jack over after all

He may have cried, just a little
trying to compare Byron's cape
to the spasm of a dying catfish
He never did get
that image just right
but Jesus Christ
his hair was *Perfect? Or was it*
the hair of a
monster?

Eat

At Schnucks a lean woman
puts low fat butter into her cart
Then at Wal-Mart a man
sneaks diet pills into his coat pocket
Later, at Denny's, I watch old folks
order from the *Fit Fare* menu

My wife looks me over before she finally says
maybe you should try something low carb

To this I say no
I will eat

I will eat with abandon and love it
as none have loved it before me
Fat will hang from my bones
in great folds. Shake like
blinds in a gale when I laugh

My fat will be an avalanche

I will wear the greasy lips of a hamburger   *Who Trump, Bird?*
eating man. I'll wipe my Cheeto stained hands   *Bird, who*
upon my sweat pants and not give a damn   *Trump?*
who's watching   *Bird, you up?*
    You up, Bird?
When I hit 1000 pounds,   *You real up?*
I'll make the talk show circuit

Well, Ellen, I don't really have any regrets. I'm a man of
many vices and all in all it's been a pretty good life. Ellen
won't believe me of course, but then again, she has to stay
thin for television

When I die, my children will have a hard time finding
a casket for me. They'll have to bust the church door
down off its hinges to fit me in.
When they sing *How Great Thou Art*
they'll be talking about Taco Bell

When people ask my wife what happened
the smile of gorged passion still wet
upon my lips will be her answer.

I Wouldn't Mind You Crazy if You Didn't Get So Damned Depressed About It

Nothing went right today
but all my problems
were small ones
ripped pants no one
showed up for the reading
fifty bucks to last two more weeks
and now doing dishes
with a beach towel
because of all the things
I forgot to wash

She's off her meds	*Who's crazy, Bird?*
We're all off our meds	*You are, Snuffy.*
and crazy inconsolable gods	*Who Trump, Bird?*
instead and someone	*You are, Snuffy.*
says who cares about	*You Trump, you Trump*
poetry anyway and I	*You Trump, Bird. How*
say I do. I love it more	*high are you, Bird?*
than almost anything	*High enough to sleep.*
and someone else says	*Good to know, Bird,*
and anything and	*Good to know.*
it goes on and on and on	
like that for a very long time.	

Dear Nerd, In Regards to Your Nerd Query

I can say with some confidence
that if I could choose one super power
it would be a cyber-tooth

Likely, I'd be the descendant
of Wolverine from some alternate
universe brought to Earth-616
by one of Reed Richard's crazy ass
experiments with the negative zone

Eventually, I'd come to see Logan
as a father figure and after much adjustment
I might even join X-Force
or some lesser known group of mutants

Unfortunately, like Wolverine
I too would have a thing for redheads
My unquenchable lust for Jean Grey
would drive me to fits of insanity

At first, the old man would have my back
but after I joined the Brotherhood of
Evil Mutants, he'd feel it necessary to
hunt me down like a wild animal

Luckily for me, my tingling cyber-tooth
would give just enough warning
for me to escape back to my own world

Sure, he'd get a few good licks in
but my mild healing factor
which I'd previously used only
for hangovers and and stumped toes
would keep me alive

Once back in my own time-line
I would be turned from my evil
ways by the love of a good woman
A woman I can only assume
would be Tiffany
of Mall rock fame

So, to answer your question
I wouldn't want Omega level
powers like the Beyonder or Thanos

Dear, God, No
Look at all the pain
I wrought
with nothing
but this stupid cyber-tooth
and low self-esteem.

> *Was that funny, Bird?*
> *Yes.*
> *You got wild ideas, Bird.*
> *Yes.*

Brutal

Let's have a gay night, he said.
A gay night?
Of course, we didn't know what he meant. I was eight and my cousin, Terry, was nine. We were staying the night with our great-aunt and our 19-year-old cousin, Larry, who lived with her. Larry was very handsome, and he could almost dunk a basketball, which went a long way with us. He also seemed to like hanging out with us. Earlier, Terry and I (who grew up in the same house) had been playing Army with him in our back yard. Larry was tall, lean, and dark-skinned. Looking back on it thirty years later, I'm surprised, and a bit upset that I remember him as being so attractive.

A gay night, he said. *We all do it. It makes us men. First, let's show our dicks to each other.*

This is where coherency ends.

What I remember are flashes—bits and pieces. Some of it, I didn't remember until a few years ago when Terry and I talked about it for the first time.

Terry and I were nervous. We laughed a lot. We finally pulled our dicks out. Larry's was hard as a rock, huge it seemed to me, surrounded by pubic hair. Terry's was just naturally big. Mine wasn't. So it, of course, became the butt of jokes for the night. It didn't help that I was fat. A little plump pig, which Larry seemed to actually like. After we'd pulled our cocks out and talked about them for a bit, Larry invited us downstairs. Our great-aunt had one of those old-fashioned exercise machines down there. One with a limp, stained belt.

Let's take turns putting our dicks on it and turning it on, Larry said. So we did. Somehow this is the worst part of it.

Has always been the worst part of it. Thinking back, which I try not to do, it's the monster in the basement. Dirty and stained. I knew even then that this was the turning point. There would be no going back after the monster. I even thought about stopping it then. Other than this, we mostly just went to church together. Larry would sit beside us, smacking green apple gum, and asking as quietly as he could which girls in church we might fuck, if we had the chance. We thought that was really cool. He'd even ask us about his sister, who I had some sort of weird, 8-year-old crush on.

 It got worse, of course. It was all about what we would do to him. Would we touch his balls? Would we take his dick in our mouth? I did. Hating it and liking it at the same time. I honestly can't remember what Terry did. I'm sure it was much the same.

 When I titled this "Brutal," I expected it to be brutal. Other than a surreal poem I wrote and published in the late 90s, this is the only thing I've ever written about that experience. The poem dealt in symbolism. I told myself, if I ever have the guts to write about it, it's going to be brutal. It's going to be honest and detailed. The details, however, are like an impressionist painting. Parts of it, like the monster, are painfully vivid. Larry's white, white teeth. His beautiful body. The rest is images, textures, feelings. Feelings of guilt and desire all mixed up in one. The taste of his cock and how I remember it being both hard and somehow soft at the same time—the way the skin of it followed my movements.

 Whenever I would think about writing this, I'd think, there's a book in it. There's not. There are just these images. Whatever else there might have been, would be about the aftermath, and I've written about that over and over again.

The next morning, I woke up naked on the living room floor. Larry had uncovered me to show his sister. She was laughing at how fat I was. Terry was already ready for church. We didn't see Larry much after that. He decided we weren't really that cool to hang out with anymore. I guess we felt the same. The next time I remember seeing him was at my brother's funeral. He was still handsome. He had rented me a movie, Better Off Dead.

There's a lot to say about my brother and how, even though he knew nothing about this, he should have done something about it, but not here. The next time I heard about Larry, he had died in motorcycle accident. My hometown, Leadwood, kills a lot of people. I was happy he was dead. I'm not sure I am anymore.

For all of his talk about a gay night, Larry wasn't gay. Some times I am. And though I consider myself to have the most bleeding heart I've ever known, child molesters still make me scream out for the death penalty. That, however, is neither here nor there. That's just me still trying to defend myself for not stopping this. For not saying no to the monster.

When I was young, and I would feel like, or people would think, I was a really fucked up person, they would think may be it was because my brother had died when I was thirteen. I'd let them. But it wasn't. It was this. This.

Terry and I were very, very drunk and in our 30s, at a bar, when I finally said something about it.

You know why were so fucked up? I asked.

Larry, he said.

I nodded.

The thing I most remembered, he said, *was Larry fucking you in the ass.*

I hadn't remembered.

You screamed like a pig, Terry said.

I remembered then. I remembered everything. Hands and knees and pain.

Elmo Goes Emo

Elmo's soul is black as obsidian
Elmo's pain is only dampened by
the jagged cuts upon
Elmo's arms

Elmo made them with a beer bottle cap

Elmo wonders who can remember
the sun
Elmo's heart torn like crepe paper

Have always hated this
The stain on Elmo cannot be washed away   *fuck knuckle.*
Not even by Tide
and Tide knows fabric best   *I like him, Bird*
I really like him.

Wind. Frigid. Cold. Winter.

Snuffleupagus has a trunk like a baseball bat

Elmo shouldn't have said that

Elmo's going to be gutted like a rat

Tickle Elmo? Please
tickle Elmo

until Elmo can't breathe.

C is for Cookie

I won't believe this is real
anymore. Like I'm going to just
lay here all night shaking, thinking again
of the cookie when there is a jar full
in the kitchen and if those are gone
a gas station just down the road

It's hard. My father loved the Oreo
and his father the macaroon. It was
good enough for them, I thought,
it's good enough for me

But cookies are what got me into this
mess, cookies are why I quiver,
but I'd known only hunger when
the chickens from my cookie eating
days finally came home to roost

The things I did all hopped up
on cookies do not suffer forgiveness

I've been a bad monster. In my endless   *This ain't the monster*
thirst maybe   *to worry about, Bird.*

I wasn't thinking straight. Maybe
she'd just given me all the forgiveness   *Stop scaring me, Snuffy.*
she had to give. Maybe it didn't matter
that I had given up cookies

because I still thought of them. I still
kept one in my desk drawer just in case   *I'd stop turning pages*
You don't have to talk when you've got   *if I were you.*
a fig newton in your mouth. There's no
room to think with a mind full of sugar

So when she asked
I cracked one wide
and a million different
fortunes spread before us

I opened my mouth to
say so but it hung
a gaping black wound

all my life I've known silence
except deep down
where it whispers
insistently
madly
finally
Cookie
Cookie
Cookie!

A Dream of Siblings

I dreamed first of my sister   *Told you not to turn the page.*

She couldn't speak
She was smiling

Young and beautiful
with long, straight red hair

She bopped me on the head
with a pen like little bunny foo foo

Then I was in a hearse
with my brother's old girlfriend

We were driving through a gray
failing city

She was young. She
tried crawling into the back seat
and I caught a glimpse of her
striped panties

Shit, I thought, this is it
another sex dream about Vicki

But it wasn't

Your brother is still alive
she said. Your parents
didn't tell you

I ask her to take me to him
He's on the top floor of an impossibly
tall apartment building

He's lying on a couch
He's covered in burn scars
His jaw is webbed skin, and I
can see his teeth and bloated tongue

He can't speak

It's been thirty years
It's me, I say. It's Dan

He weeps. He moans. He
tries to move, but can't
Pain and silent pleading

When I wake
I can't help but wonder
if this was a message from
the afterlife

My sister, so devout,
happy, impish

and the pen?

I don't know.

My brother who
carried a gun under the front
seat of his truck who died
driving drunk

in some kind of hell

Even though I gave up
believing in this shit
years ago, I still wonder

Maybe I never gave up believing

Maybe, once having faith, no one
ever gives up believing

Even if the things we believe in
are horrifying.

City of Bones
the worst thing we've ever seen
Robert Bowcock, environmental investigator and colleague of Erin
Brockovich (Speaking of Leadwood, Missouri)

I.

The bones broken
bleached cages
just down the street
the new weeds grow
a strange green

The solution to cover lead
with more lead from a town
not much better off than we are

When that didn't work they
sprayed it down with sewage

It's safe, they promised

and the bones grew to dandelions
and we were thankful

to find femurs, ribs bent
to smiles, bits of teeth
tumors spreading into
the marrow of our lives

The shit brought in from the Livestock
Sale Barn, the port-o-potty company
full of hypodermic needles biting

and then

Well, and then there was nothing
not even the sound of our cancers
Only the weight of lead
in our blood and minds

This is what our fathers died for
we said

II.

I said
The Company left us
here where the chat dumps loom
like tombstones
Left us like pigs without tits to suck
I said
The Company decided
lead was no longer viable
and left us with it, an illness
I said
an illness
We're all so very sick
it doesn't really matter anymore
what the men in suits from safer cities
say I said
When they got around to it
they hauled in dirt with less lead
to cover what we already had
and when that didn't work
they covered our town in
literal shit

Months later we were still
picking out bones and teeth
from the dirt
In some yards after the rain
had washed it away
we were left with piles of bones
        cattle they said
it's safe and the needles
no one is ill, no one is sick

Our grandfather's won't speak of it
won't utter an ill word toward The Company
that fed them
gave them something to do with their
backs and hands

III.

What I really mean is this:
        the lead runs deep
        the dark waters
        the tumored fish
        the rough hands
        run deep

        Robbie killed himself
        Mike killed himself
        Buck killed himself
        on and on

It's so simple
our town is small
there's no money

IV.

We live in shit
We vote Republican
We pound our Bibles
Eat at Macdonald's
drive big trucks
We drink a lot
we fight a lot
we fuck a lot
and pray a lot for salvation

The lady across the street
finally took down her Jesus
is coming soon sign

There's glory in the blood *So sayeth Elmo*

We were all so busy
waiting on Armageddon
we never noticed
it was already here.

I Don't Write Political Poems (On the Eve of a Government Shutdown)

We fed our kids
fish sticks
and we ate corn dogs
We knew it was poison

Sometimes we didn't eat

My mother fed me fat noodles
in watered-down tomato sauce
covered in spices from a plastic bottle

After three or four days
I imagined them worms
writhing in blood

In sixth grade
I had a cough for six months
but my only doctor trip
was for scabies

They itched in hard
red welts, living there
They were contagious
a poor people problem

My grandmother
read us the Bible at night instead
instead of what
no one ever said

I don't write political poems because
I'm no expert
on the economy or budgets
or cost cutting
measures

I *am* an expert
on being poor
of making a box of Kraft
Macaroni and Cheese stretch
like bloody fingers across a white
plate in a white apartment

There's some money now
and we give what we can
or so we say
but when I'm writing this
there's electricity, T.V,
an open can of Diet Coke
half-empty and flat
that I'll throw away

How many people
could I feed on what I
spend on Diet Coke

A number

Still others wait
while I wonder what
could have been done
with all the money

spent on beer
and whiskey
and cigarettes
all the cool poet tricks

Still others
hoard cash
in the name of Jesus
but it's hard to eat a tank
and bullets don't make good doctors

Sometimes the noodles had hamburger
most of the time they didn't
Out of habit, my sister waited
to go to the doctor
and now it's too late

> *Let's shut her down, boys!*

    I see my mother standing
    in front of an open window
    It's summer
    She's wringing a dishtowel
    dry in her hands.

My Mother Calls

and says I need
to visit my sister
soon

My first thoughts
are selfish ones

No one tells me
anything

because I took my brother's
death so badly as a boy

But I'm a grown man now
in middle-age
only a few years
younger than

the sister who used
to spank me with
a giant metal spoon

or better yet
pretend to so that
I didn't get a real
beating

Mom says:
> She's on so much pain
> medication now
> she doesn't always
> know where she's
> at

I feel the ground
under my feet
soaked with lead

I feel the last
aging child
heavy on the heart
of my mother

I make plans
with my wife
and daughters
to visit
and all
the
anger
in
Leadwood, Missouri
wells up
right
here
in the
final

line

of
this
goddamned
poem

The true story
of Leadwood, Missouri is this:

the ground that waits
the blood heavy with lead
the cigarettes we smoked
and beers we drank
the bullets we shot
the bibles we kept
the big company bucks
someone
somewhere
makes.

Spirit Animal: Margot Tenenbaum

I'm walking home from the bar
and the thought races *We just call it*
I've puked but there is more beer *the thought*
at home I'm already looking *now? That's*
forward to *rich.*

A young man runs by me
talking into a headset
Yes sir, he says, don't
you stop breathing on me

He runs out in front *We do.*
of a car, nearly gets hit
before I can ask if he needs help
he's in the darkness, still
running

I always cry when it *It's a stupid*
gets to the part where *movie, cuck.*
the guy says
It's been a rough year, Dad

Partly because I have two
daughters and I can imagine *Who gives a fuck?*
them saying that to me

Partly because I had a father
and cannot imagine saying it to him

We were good Missouri people
As for feelings, we were mostly
against them

Margaret's
family is a carnival and

We've had days that were hell
and days that were not   *More hell, wouldn't*
                                                  you say?

I say, Margot Tenenbaum
is my spirit animal
I guess that makes you The Baumer

I'm more like the Ben Stiller
character, she says   *Elmo want scissors!*

I think I need help, I say
Me too, she says.   *Me say Cookie!*

Welcome to Fantasy Island

You are either God or a god
in your angel suit
I saw you make life from nothing

You even fought the Devil once
who, as I always suspected,
looked just like Roddy McDowall

Offer us love
offer us redemption
I dare you

No one's fantasy is ever
I ran out of weed
I'm too fat
I have cancer
My husband is a real asshole

A quick perusal of craigslist
shows that most fantasies have
nothing to do with dancing with
the late great Sammy Davis Jr.
finding love or
a child
but mostly have to do with nipple clamps
and bodily fluids

And you can't just give anyone their fantasy

Instead, it's a week of devastating
psychological torture
only to find that
our fantasies were within us
all along if we'd just
been able to see them

I briefly entertained the idea
that your island was sponsored by
the Koch brothers as a way
to convince poor people
they never really had it as bad
off as they thought

But, I've never seen any poor
people on Fantasy Island

I only see rich people
mostly white
I assume they
are Republicans

Then again, if you *are* God
why haven't any of them
freaked out about your Latin Heritage?

Why hasn't Fox News declared Fantasy Island
a war on blue-eyed Jesus?

What the hell is Tattoo?

I need to know

By the time it's over
by the time you're done
toying with us
everyone wants off
this island

Even me. And I believe in
you, Mr. Rourke. I do. *You don't.*

Don't Kill Self

I had been walking for over 45 minutes
when I realized I was on the wrong street
Then I thought
Does it mean something?

I stood there awhile
Earlier, I was very high
and I kept saying to myself
I'm going to kill myself tomorrow   *Find that needle*
I'm going to kill myself tomorrow   *in the hay yet?*
just like that movie

Then on the way home
some drunk college girl said   *Don't worry. The*
why are you in a tie   *monster at the end of*
is this fucking wall street   *at the end of this book*
or something   *will find it for you.*

And it was all fine
until something lurched
in my back.

Jazz

I don't like it
I never know when
to clap

I'm supposed to like it
appreciate it
dig it
but words
get buried
bone deep

If Jazz is so goddamned good
why did Jack Kerouac feel
the obsessive need to talk
over it to
drink through it to
never sing it

On karaoke night
I walk into the bar
and find a fucking jazz band

and the drums
are crazy
a strange and beautiful
ending

I'm alone. I talk
to the bartender
when I can
The only
rhythm in this place is OCD

I don't realize I'm in
the middle of a cliché until an old
man sits next to me

A close-talker
His breath smells
like vomit

The drums are a wicked
rebuke. An apocalyptic
god mouth

I know that doesn't make
sense sometimes
you string a few words together
just to get lost in them

The old guy tells the bartender
a homophobic joke
He meanders. It
takes too long
The punchline is stumbling
home

but when he gets there
it's something about why
you can't put a missing gay
kid's picture on a carton of
milk anymore

Everybody gets offended
by the word homo

And bisexuals he says
you have to put their face
on a carton of half and half

Then I'm thinking half and half
half and half, over and over
like it's complex

For a moment there's relief
and I remind myself that in
all the billions of years
one could have been alive
1995 was a pretty good one

The drums are
not quite my footsteps
two hours in the future
walking home—
but something like it
something close to it
something that sounds like it
half the beautiful and strange
sound of it

When the bartender walks away
the sax sounds manic and blue
all at once and

I nearly die when all the pretty
people in their nice coats clap

Pukey leans in close
asks if I swing to the right
I don't know what that means
I say

He ask where I come from
When I say Leadwood,
he says well son of a bitch
me too you son of a bitch

I turn my face away
I can't stand the smell
like a rotting possum
like lead
like my dead dad

All I do is nod and nod and nod

He says, You heard of the committee of 300?
I nod
He says, How about the Bilderberg group?
I nod

Six people control everything, he says
the Queen of England is one of them

I nod, but
I'm thinking
strange and beautiful
thoughts
like half and half and half and

Then the other thoughts pound
it out
It's not real, I think

My mind has turned on me
I know that
everything is off
the light
the stove
my computer

Jazz wasn't built for alcohol

They want to give me pills
Blame it on the Bilderberg group
I guess
blame it on the half and half
blame it on the rain or neurons that fire
like guns blame it on this motherfucker
or what I'm
going to do tomorrow

I can't stop hearing it

The old man is here still
his breath like vomit

The future is here
It's breath and sound
stumbling home
He's not just homophobic
and racist. He may be insane
or on something

Do I feel sorry for him? Can I?
Can empathy stretch like veins
for miles

if you cut open your arm
pull them free
can they reach the moon just
like JFK said?

I guess so
I guess so

Still, I can't stand the smell
I can't stand the rain
blame it on whatever you want

I pay up. I walk home alone.
My breath is fog, my footsteps
a wavering heart

my thoughts a beat

I'm going to kill myself tomorrow
I'm going to kill myself tomorrow
I'm going to kill myself tomorrow

George Bailey's Blues

Mania starts like this:
You want to travel
Anywhere will do

You want to build
the biggest buildings   *Yuge!*
and best bridges

Most of all
you want out
of Bedford Falls and
away from that goddamn
Building and Loan

You might fall in love
Maybe with Mary
Maybe with Violet
Maybe with both

After it wears off
you are numbed
like everything is
in black and white
and wading through
snow

Day after day
it's just you
and fucking Uncle
Billy

It gets so boring
you've just got to ruin
everything. Or at least
Uncle Billy does

Of course
then depression sinks in

It's a bad one
So bad
the delusions begin

You decide to jump
off a bridge about
8 feet above the water
Serious? A cry
for help? Does it matter?

The next thing you know
you're talking to people
who ain't there and
you see the town for what it really is

A bunch of mean drunks and strip malls

But like all the October decorations
and that stupid Starbucks' cup
it won't stop there

The whole damn thing
starts again
Your new obsession
is bells

No one is sure
if *Uncle Billy*
ever even existed.

*Worse things than you can imagine
exist, Bird. Grump, Trump, Devil,
the bomb, insurance. And finally
a monster you can't even imagine.*

Full Moon

I'm in the dog food aisle
at Wal-Mart when I
am told that my sister
is going to die
It's near Christmas

I run
into my mother

Well, she says   *I don't want to be in*
                                                  this poem, Danny

Your sister has
lung cancer
and there's nothing
that can be done about it

She's found Jesus
but when it was in
her throat
and they thought
it was gone
after the surgery
they called it a miracle   *A Christmas Miracle!*

This will be the
second child my
mother loses   *I said no!*

A lot of people
die early here

Tonight, I smoke a joint
I step out on the back porch
I try to imagine the woods
behind my house as death
a passage to the other side
even with a full moon it's dark. *You have no idea.*

I'm Going to Kill Myself Tomorrow
By The Ghost Nipples
(Natty and Cracker, music and lyrics)

(Capo on 1st fret)

Am   Em

I'm going to kill myself tomorrow

Am   Em

I'm going to kill myself tomorrow

C   D   Am

I'm fucking serious.
I'm going to do it tomorrow.

Repeat as necessary, Bird

I Like To Cut Myself
By The Ghost Nipples
(Natty and Cracker, music and lyrics)

G
Some people like airplanes

C
others like shelves

G
me, I like to cut myself

G
Some people like Santa

C
and Christmas and elves

G
but me, I like to cuuuuut myself

C
Some people like Elvis

G
Nobody likes a mess

Let's do something, Snuffy
I don't feel like it, Bird.
We've got to got to got to.
Let's go to a bar. Let's fuck a lady. Or a guy, I don't care but come on come on.

Elmo knows what to do.

C
except for me when I'm cuuuuting myself

> *I like this kid, Bird. He's got*
> *the right idea. Get the hell*
> *out of here before it's too*
> *late.*

G
Everyone likes ice cream

C
but no one likes me

G
so a cutting it willl beeeeeeeeeeeeeeeee

The Normals

I mean you and
I mean it
as a derogatory

I'm not blaming you
and your normal thoughts
your normal moods your
normal sex drives and
normal wives

Your normal views
bother me
Everything bothers me
especially your ugly
normal children

Do they even listen?

God made me a poet
and made you a monster   *Deplorable*

Stupid fucking normals
your lives fit like a shoe
Every morning I take a pill
so that I can be just like
stupid fucking ugly you.

*Listen to me, you mania
tainted asshole. Stop turning pages.
We're the
same, really? Aren't we
really the same, Bird? All
of us here? So, please, stop.*

Pill

The next time you see me
I'll be dead
You won't know it
I won't know it
but it'll be true

I'll look the same
mostly sound the same
you may think I even
seem better
but it won't
be me.
                       hahahahahhahahhahhahahahhahahahh
                       hahaahahahahhahaha

Elton and George

The first time I kissed a man
we were at a straight party
alone in the kitchen
grabbing beers

The Elton John and George Michael
version of *Don't Let the Sun Go
Down on Me* came on the radio

We started to sing along
moving closer to
each other
hands clenched close
to our mouths
holding invisible
microphones

Something older than
Kentucky rain fell
between us

Then we kissed
full-tongued

We had to be careful
getting caught risked a beating

It was like something
out of a goddamned movie

It was then I knew gay men
are better in both style and substance
at almost everything

The rest of the story
isn't so cute

It was 1991
We were falling
in love in a small
town in Missouri

and two years later
he'd be dead
found hanged in his room
because, after all,
this was a small town
in Missouri in 1991.

Take a Moment

to think about the damage
you've caused
The lives you've fucked
over

Remember, for a moment
every lie you've told

For just a minute
stop telling people
how much better you
are now

that there's a pill for you

You hid so well
remember that

You don't need
to hide anymore.

I've remembered all
these things and more
today

Then went back to finish
the pans I'd left to soak
in the kitchen.

I Wish

to write my poems
across your body

Long, Whitmanesque lines
up your calves and into your thighs

A series of haiku linked
across one cheek
to the next

Something like William
Carlos Williams might write
upon your breasts

A bald confession scrawled
over your face

Typical drunken ramblings
like any poet might
from shoulder blade to
shoulder blade

There goes the poet's wife
people will say

What lovely lines

But look at her face
What has her husband
done today

I told you poets
were no good

How can someone have
so much to say about a left arm

Who stamps a poem onto
an earlobe

They'll find it sweet and scandalous
mad and misogynistic

Only you'll know the words
mean nothing
anchors you'll treat as balloons

and who doesn't love a balloon?

> *Fuck you, Bird. Fuck you fuck*
> *you and fuck you and fuck you.*

In Response to the Article "10 People to Rid Yourself of Before the New Year"

Leave them behind
The wounded, the addicted
the fucked up

The cheaters, the liars
and the motherfuckers

The bastards, the bitches
the mentally ill

The pill poppers, the drunks
the cutters and the out and out
pieces of shit

Give them to me. These
are the people I want

The humans, the disconnected
the holy rollers

All of these beautiful sons
and daughters

Everyone who has given up

I'll take each and every one

It's going to be all right, I'll say
Shhh, everything
is going to be all right.

> *You really wanted that to be the end of the book, didn't you?*
> *I did, Snuffy.*
> *This isn't Snuffy. Snuffy is dead. Slit his own fucking throat.*
> *Who this? Trump?*
> *Pill's wearing off isn't it, Bird? Insurance isn't going to pay for it anyway.*
> *It still might.*
> *It won't, you stupid fucking bird. It' won't.*
> *And now?*

Dinged

They say the earth vibrates　　　　　　*You were warned.*
a remnant from being dinged
by an asteroid or two before　　　　　　*Snuffy?*
memory was invented

They say we can't feel it
but I swear to god I can
under foot—ringing
like a plate dropped without
breaking in the kitchen

But the world won't　　　　　　*Told you. Snuffy's dead.*
just crack open, will it
won't just open wide, split
will it

I have fears
and enemies everywhere

There's the goddamn email　　　　　　*Trump Trump Trump?*
The Shadow men
The Mandela Effect

All these superstitions
like straightening empty
beer bottles at the bar until

they barely touch
like reluctant lovers

She moves over to turn
them, to make sure the
labels face the same direction

and there they are
a little army   *Last chance, Crocker.*

Sometimes you need
a women who'll help you
straighten bottles

So you can say
I like the way you
straighten them bottles, mama

And sometimes you need
a woman who'll knock them down
Kill with a fist

But no on can do both, right?
That's something no one can do.

And if they start to fall
that's all right

No one can feel us vibrating

No one knows we're about
to split wide open full
of lava and lice

I mean, as long as we're funny, right?
As long as we say funny things

no one will know we're
about to crack
like an egg full
of spiders

Will they?   *Well fuck us. You're really*
                                    going to do it.

She moves over to turn
them, to make sure the
labels face the same direction

and there they are
a little army   *Last chance, Crocker.*

Sometimes you need
a women who'll help you
straighten bottles

So you can say
I like the way you
straighten them bottles, mama

And sometimes you need
a woman who'll knock them down
Kill with a fist

But no on can do both, right?
That's something no one can do.

And if they start to fall
that's all right

No one can feel us vibrating

No one knows we're about
to split wide open full
of lava and lice

I mean, as long as we're funny, right?
As long as we say funny things

no one will know we're
about to crack
like an egg full
of spiders

Will they? *Well fuck us. You're really*
going to do it.

You Better Fucking Believe There's a Monster at the End of This Book

So you've written a poem about every
goddamned person on this street but me?
Is that about right?
I know my book was scary, but come on
I tried to warn you. Don't turn the page
There's a monster at the end of this book
Did I look like I was kidding?

But you had to keep going

Well, buddy, I hope you're happy
because there's more. That's right
turn those pages, asshole
Look here, that's the birth
of Grover's daughter. On page 28
we'll relive Grover's DWI
Page 45? That's my mid-life crisis

Keep going and you'll see my struggle
with existentialism. Grover had a hell
of a divorce

The name of the monster at the end
of this book is cancer. It's addiction. It's
page after page of boredom and self-doubt

It's time you stop blaming me
If you could have, even once,
just stopped, practiced even a modicum of
self-control, you
would have never come to that
bulbous nose, those longing eyes,
that blue fur, even now, sprouting
across the compass of your body

You'd never have had to weep at the sounds
of your own wavering voice.

Daniel Crocker's work has appeared in *The Los Angeles Review, Hobart, Big Muddy, New World Writing, Stirring, Juked, The Chiron Review, The Mas Tequila Review* and over 100 others. His books include *Like a Fish* (full length) and *The One Where I Ruin Your Childhood* (e-chap with thousands of downloads) both from Sundress Publications. Green Bean Press published serveral of his books in the '90s and early 2000s. These include *People Everyday and Other Poems, Long Live the 2 of Spades,* the novel *The Cornstalk Man* and the short story collection *Do Not Look Directly Into Me.* He has also published several chapbooks through various presses. He is the editor of *The Cape Rock* (Southeast Missouri State University) and the co-editor of *Trailer Park Quarterly.* He's also the host of the podcast, *Sanesplaining,* about poetry, mental illness and nerd stuff.